GRAHAM -
World's Fastest Blind Man!

by Mark Wheeller

*Developed from **Race To Be Seen**
by Mark Wheeller and Epping Youth Theatre*

GRAHAM - World's Fastest Blind Man!
by Mark Wheeller

GRAHAM - World's Fastest Blind Man! was developed from Mark Wheeller's stage play *Race To Be Seen* written with the Epping Youth Theatre. *Race To Be Seen* was published by the Epping Forest District Council in 1984 and by Longmans in 1986.

Author's acknowledgments:
All the sources for kind permission to use their words.
The writing and researching team from Epping Youth Theatre 1983: Matthew Allen; Lisa Beer; Zara Chapman; Frances Jackson; Barold Sapsford. *They were assisted by*: Dawn Baker; Bernadette Chapman; Laura Dove; Jan Farringdon; Nicki Harris; Jonathan Hicks; Rebecca Mallison; Paddy Mallison; Luke Nyman; Sara Record; Alis Stylianou; Tracy Tee & Steve Wyatt.
Thanks to the BBC for their kind permission to use the out-take from Radio 4's *In Touch* programme. Also to Linsey Firkser (interviewer) and Tony Shearman (producer) 1999.
Tim Ford for his creative ideas and a wonderful first production.
Meg Davis at MBA Literary Agency and Evie Efthimiou at dbda for continued belief and support.

Sources:
Graham and Marie Salmon; Maud and Harry, Graham's mum and dad; June and Susan, Graham's sisters.
The following in alphabetical order: Bill Aitken; John Anderson; John Bailey; Christine Baker (Christiev Services); Mark Barratt; Mike Brace; Claude Charman; Daily Mail; Sandy Gray; Guardian and Gazette (Walthamstow); The Guinness Book of Records; Brigitte Hall; Frank Matthews; Moorfield's Eye Hospital; Ron Murray; Kath and Lew Pegg; Susie Rothwell; Joyce Streetin; Jim Weller; Keith Wells, Roger Wray and Pete Young.

Photographs:
Maud Salmon, page 6; Illustrated London News (Daily Sketch), page 6; Strat Mastoris, Page 6; Mark Wheeller, pages 6 and 64. Others from the family's collection.

GRAHAM - World's Fastest Blind Man! was premiered by the Eastleigh Borough Youth Theatre at the Edinburgh Festival Fringe, 2001.

Published by **dbda**, Pin Point, 1-2 Rosslyn Crescent, Harrow HA1 2SB.

ISBN 1 902843 09 6

BRITISH LIBRARY CATALOGUING IN PUBLICATION DATA
A catalogue record for this book is available from the British Library.

© Mark Wheeller & Marie Salmon, 2001.
The moral right of the author has been asserted.

No part of this publication may be transmitted, stored in a retrieval system or reproduced in any form or by means electronic, mechanical, photocopying, typescript, recording or otherwise, without prior permission of the copyright owners.
Photocopying of scripts is illegal! Even if you hold a licence from the Copyright Licensing Agency you are only allowed to photocopy up to a total of 5% of the whole script. Please remember the writers who depend upon their share of your purchases... without them the plays which you perform could not have been written or published.

All enquiries regarding all rights associated with this pay, including performing rights, should be addressed to:
Meg Davis, MBA Literary Agents Limited, 62 Grafton Way, London W1P 5LD.
Tel: 020 7387 2076   Fax: 020 7387 2042   E-mail: meg@mbalit.co.uk

Further copies of this publication can be purchased from:
dbda, Pin Point, 1-2 Rosslyn Crescent, Harrow HA1 2SB.
Tel: 0870 333 7771   Fax: 0870 333 7772   E-mail: dbda@dbda.co.uk

In loving memory of Graham, my "storybookman".

Mark Wheeller

Introduction

I have been privileged to interview a host of genuine sporting superstars: Muhammad Ali...Martina Navratilova... Nadia Comaneci... Tommie Smith, the 'Black Power' athlete from the 1968 Mexico Olympics... Sir Gary Sobers... John McEnroe... Pele... but I have never met anyone quite so remarkable as Graham Salmon.

Graham never considered himself a blind athlete; he was an athlete who happened to be blind. He wanted to be an Olympian, so he skied for Britain in the inaugural Winter Paralympics... he wanted to be a runner, so he went out and broke the 100 and 400 metres world records... he wanted to play golf, so he became good enough to beat the Americans at Wentworth in the Stewart Cup (the Ryder Cup for the blind)... he wanted to play cricket, so he appeared in an exhibition match at Lord's during the lunch interval of an England-Australia Test match... he wanted to be an inspiration to blind children, so he came to be awarded the MBE... he wanted to learn the Fosbury Flop, so he developed into an international class high-jumper... he wanted a new challenge, so he ran - and completed - the London Marathon and then tragically was forced to surrender his left leg to the cancer which had deprived him of both eyes as a baby.

"You've put on a bit of weight", I informed him once while leafing through the scrapbooks of his extraordinary sporting career. "I'm exactly the same weight today as I was back then", he told me in mock outrage, "ten-and-a-half stones... I'm missing a leg, of course, but my weight has remained steady."

Blessed with a 100-megawatt smile which could light up a room and send the heart soaring, Graham attacked each and every new day like a child breathlessly unwrapping their presents on Christmas morning. "Although I went to a boarding school for the blind, my parents refused to allow me to behave like a blind child and so I was encouraged to try everything all the other kids did. But when I left school, physically and mentally handicapped youngsters were expected to throw bean-bags at one another for exercise. The whole thing was a joke, a cruel joke in this country.

GRAHAM - World's Fastest Blind Man!

"No-one had any idea what blind athletes wanted. At the first multi-disabled World Championships at Stoke Mandeville, the 100 metres was run on concrete which was bad enough. But if you're trying to listen out to the voice of your caller who's guiding you and suddenly another voice over the tannoy booms out: 'Will the competitors in the paraplegic table-tennis competition please report to the main hall...!', I don't need to tell you what happens. The 100 metres runners were hurtling all over the place. I think two nearly drowned in the steeplechase water-jump..."

Mark Wheeller has captured the very essence of Graham Salmon in this most moving of plays; his courage, his dignity, his sense of humour but, above all, his overwhelming love of life.

Robert Philip
Daily Telegraph Sports Columnist

Production Notes:

The production should be presented simply, yet imaginatively.
Few props are required together with a composite set.
The play is divided into sections as opposed to scenes.
One section should flow into the next thus preventing stop/start scene changes.
Physical realisation of feelings, actions and items are to be encouraged. This will also serve to involve the supporting cast in all of the scenes. Ideally, they will be on stage, actively involved throughout the play. There is a danger that a play with narrators can become static... please do all you can to avoid this!

Good luck to all who work on this very personal play.

GRAHAM - The World's Fastest Blind Man!

Top left:
Graham as a baby - the photo his parents wanted the day before he had the operation to remove his eye. "We wanted a photo of him, to remember what he looked like... before they did it. That was important to us."

Bottom left:
Graham set a new British high jump record for the totally blind at 1 metre 38... about neck height to an average adult.

Top right:
Graham on his tricycle proudly posing for the local newspaper.

Bottom right:
Graham training for the 1983 European Championships with his guide, Roger Wray.

List of Characters

Male 1:   Graham

Male 2:   Mark

Male 3:   Harry

Male 4:   Ron; John; Pete; RNIB Officer; Personnel Officer 1; Client; Roger

Male 5:   Mr Mason; Claude; Headteacher; Teacher; RNIB Employment Officer; Jim; John Anderson

Female 1:   Marie

Female 2:   Maud

Female 3:   Producer; Junie; Madge; Deanne; Woman; Personnel Officer 2; Marion; Official

Female 4:   Susan; Bystander; Personnel Officer 3; Susie; Announcer

---

Cast of First Performance - Directed by Tim Ford:

Alex Morgan Jones - Graham
Amy Dwyer/Emily Hartman - Marie
Patrick Harris - Harry
Helen Cole - Maud
Matt Beames - Mark
Sarah Bell - Junie/Chorus
Neil Brabant - Ron/Chorus
Laura Whiting - Susan/Chorus
Lee Griffiths - John/Chorus

Tara Whiting - Sound & Set
Lighting - Matt Williams
Administration - Christine Farleigh & Julie Edwards

Section 1   A Race to be Seen... Introducing Graham

In the first production of this play the director incorporated Mark (along with the "chorus") into the scenes that Graham was describing... and also incorporated Graham (along with the chorus) into the scenes that Mark describes. This integration worked brilliantly and created a fluidity and opportunity for more movement than static narrator figures offer... please avoid Mark (or Graham) as static narrators at all costs!

SONG 1:   **RACE TO BE SEEN**

(This opening song is optional.[1] If it is used it could be sung by "Mark" or an entirely separate singer/choral group. Slides[2] of Graham in sports kit/with medals could be shown during this song.)

Mark:
*There's a race at the national stadium... all tickets have been sold.
The world's top runners will be there... trying to take the gold.
Their determination each to win mean that...
We will witness a race to be seen.*

Mark, Marie & Graham:
*There's a race at the local running track... no tickets to be sold.
There'll be no famous runners there... there'll be no winner's gold.
But their determination to succeed will surely mean
That they will be part of... a race to be seen.*

All:
*Like the runners... we're all part of a race.
Some days you win... some days you fall.
But if you never help yourself... then you'll never win at all.
If you spend your life just dreaming... success won't come to you.
Race to be seen and show the world what you can do!*

Graham:
*There's a race we should all attempt to win... but we don't always try.
If we give up hope for the future now... this race of ours will die.*

---

(1) CDs of the songs from GRAHAM are available from dbda, Pin Point, 1-2 Rosslyn Crescent, Harrow HA1 2SB. Tel: 0870 333 7771   Fax: 0870 333 7772   E-mail: dbda@dbda.co.uk

(2) These slides are available from MBA Literary Agents Ltd., 62 Grafton Way, London W1P 5LD. Tel: 020 7387 2076   Email: meg@mbalit.co.uk

GRAHAM - World's Fastest Blind Man!

Graham, Mark & Marie:	*For life is like a relay... we have our lap to run* *Don't drop the baton... it's worth handing on!*
All:	*Like the runners... we're all part of a race.* *Some days you win... some days you fall.* *But if you never help yourself... then you'll never win at all.* *If you spend your life just dreaming...success won't come to you.* *Race to be seen and show the world what you can do!* *Race to be Seen.*
Mark:	February 1979: My tutor at Goldsmiths College, in London, told me that **Boney M**... a top pop group of the time, wanted to record a song I'd just written on their new album! I was over the moon... this was it... I'm going to be a star! Meanwhile... down the road at Crystal Palace... Graham Salmon, who I would go on to meet some four years later, was participating in the Southern Counties Three A's Open Meeting. On the face of it, nothing very exceptional... certainly not compared to the prospect of a hit single... but listen. *(Graham enters, dressed in a tracksuit and wearing dark glasses, which are only removed for races.)* Graham had been totally blind, pretty much from birth. He was running, unaccompanied, against fully sighted athletes. His coach, Ron Murray, *(Ron enters)* was to be at the end of the track shouting directions ...
Ron:	*(Shouting as though in the race)* Right a bit Graham... right... right!!!
Mark:	... to ensure Graham maintained a straight line. Imagine running a race in front of a big crowd like this... and being the only competitor forced to wear a blindfold? Would you be up for it?
Ron:	It was a bitterly cold day.
Mark:	*(Laugh)* I think the weather would've probably put me off!
Marie:	The snow was thick.
Mark:	*(Introducing Marie to the audience.)* Graham and his wife, Marie, *(pronounced Mahrie)* made their way to the restaurant to meet up with Ron.

Section 1

	(The scene from here should be pacey with actors involving themselves in "business" to convey the frantic activity of those referred to.)
Graham:	After a quick cup of tea we went to the undercover area to warm up.
Ron:	Jogging to get the blood circulating
Graham:	Then exercises to loosen the joints and stretch every muscle.
Ron:	The indoor area was packed with athletes making their final preparations.
Mark:	The press were there.
Graham:	I loved the attention...
Marie:	There were hundreds of photographers.
All:	Click. *(A freeze frame.)*
Ron:	The BBC were setting up cameras near the track.
Marie:	With a dispatch rider ready to rush the film of the race up in time to show on that evening's nine o'clock news.
Mark:	The newsmen were after a sensation.
Marie:	They wanted Graham to win.
Ron:	We had no way of telling how good the opposition might be.
Graham:	My nerves were on edge... my heart pumping with excitement.
Ron:	I was saying "try to relax" but I was as nervous as he was.
Graham:	The tension gripped me.
All:	To your marks.
Marie:	Good luck Gray.
Mark:	This was it... his first race against sighted runners.
Marie:	There would be no quarter asked... and none given.
All:	Set!

GRAHAM - World's Fastest Blind Man!

Graham: I sensed my chance for glory, but feared the prospect of disaster. I took a deep breath and held it!
(Silence)

All: Bang!!!

Ron: Come on Graham - drive! Lift your knees higher. Drive with your arms.

Mark: He could hear the man on his right edging in front.

Ron: Right a bit Graham... Right! Right! Right!

Mark: Obeying Ron's instruction he altered his course slightly.

Ron: Faster! Faster! Stay with him! Faster!
(All cheer. Pause. Graham regains his composure and gets his breath back.)

Graham: The applause was thunderous as I crossed the line. I hadn't won... but I'd proved that running alone against fully sighted athletes could be done. I enjoyed the elation, but already I was planning the next race... this time I'd win!

Ron: This pioneering initiative inspired clubs to include events for the visually handicapped in their own meetings.

Graham: Thankfully my parents, teachers and friends had always allowed my competitive nature to flourish... without it I may never have won an important victory... that of acceptance.

Mark: So... groundbreaking events for Graham Salmon in February 1979... but not so with Boney M and my song. I still don't know whether it was all one big wind up. I heard nothing more about it.[3]
Graham built on his success running in many more Open Meetings against sighted athletes. Those I witnessed, a few years later, figure as <u>the</u> most exciting sporting events I have ever seen. I loved the seemingly impossible challenge of a blind man taking on fully sighted athletes.

Graham: It was brilliant... I knew everybody'd be shocked!

Mark: It really gave people something to talk about.

---

[3] The song EYES OF A CHILD eventually became the finale for Mark Wheeller's Musical BLACKOUT.

Section 1

Ron: In the 400 metre races Graham ran with a guide because of the bends... linked by a 16 inch length of string.*(4)*

Graham: They always put us in the outside lanes... well out of the way... I don't know what they imagined we'd do... maybe they thought we'd have to go round strangling people to win the race!

Mark: I remember the first race I saw... there were two boys in the crowd laughing... taking the mick... I seriously considered going over and "having a word"... but, as I was to see, Graham didn't need me or anyone to fight his corner. As the race finished the two laughing boys ran up to Graham and got his autograph.

I met Graham, and Marie, in 1982. I was a young Youth Theatre director and wanted to develop a play, with the Epping Youth Theatre, celebrating the achievements of someone local. I knew very little about Graham when we first met... he knew nothing about EYT and me.

The resultant play, *Race To Be Seen*, was created from a jigsaw of extensive interviews. This documentary style would, we hoped, get as close to Graham, as words would allow. I once worked out that our hard working Youth Theatre research group handwrote over fifteen hundred A4 sheets of interview transcripts. We used only these words to make the script... we were very strict about this self-imposed rule. We wanted it to be authentic. *Race To Be Seen* went on to win accolades at the Edinburgh Festival Fringe and became my first published script. Graham and I developed a lasting friendship... I was very proud to have him as my Best Man when I married Rachel and, with Marie, he proved a wonderful Godparent to our children.

Much happened to Graham after *Race To Be Seen* and this is my attempt at a more complete and updated portrait of an amazing athlete... and a very special friend.

Ron: Graham represented Great Britain at every major athletics competition between 1977 and 1987. He broke records in the 100 metres, the 400 metres, and the high jump.

---

(4) These slides are available from MBA Literary Agents Ltd. See Footnote 2.

GRAHAM - World's Fastest Blind Man!

	He ski'd for Britain in the Winter Para Olympics, and played cricket at Lords.
Mark:	When he retired from athletics he did the Marathon, so I was not surprised when he phoned to tell me about his involvement in a sport that would win him even more publicity.
Graham:	Chingford Golf Range 're going to let me join.
Mark:	Not only that... but he'd asked Gordon Goldie, a professional there, to coach him. Most people would learn the basics with a friend and then get professional help... not Graham...
Graham:	Gordon reckons he'll be able to teach me the perfect swing... because I haven't ever seen anyone play.
Mark:	This epitomised Graham's approach... and his "handicap" tumbled faster than Isaac Newton's famous apple. Within a year Graham was in the British team! The year after that, his was the first name on the team sheet! Then... the phone call that topped it all!
Graham:	*(Speaking into a telephone.)* You won't believe this...
Mark:	Surely nothing Graham could do would surprise me...
Graham:	I've just got back from the British Open...
Mark:	I made a stab at the obvious guess... "You won?"
Graham:	I hit a hole in one!
Mark:	What?
Graham:	They're doing a piece about it on the Big Breakfast tomorrow morning.
Mark:	It defied belief!
Graham:	I didn't think so! I went straight to the bookies to get odds on doing it again!
Mark:	I used to call Graham "Storybook Man"... his life was full of remarkable experiences and achievements... in 1989 all this was recognised. He was awarded the MBE.

Section 1

	Unfortunately my Storybook Man was equally acquainted with tragedy. Cancer, which had caused his blindness as a baby struck again... a year after the hole in one, and, four years after overcoming Hairy Cell Leukaemia, Graham had some dreadful news to impart...
Graham:	*(Speaking into a telephone.)* Mark... it's Graham. *(Silence)* I've got some very grave news.
Mark:	I remember him saying the word "grave"... I remember thinking what an unusual choice of word.
Graham:	They've got to take my leg away.
Mark:	He'd been having problems with his leg... but this was Graham Salmon... surely whatever it was he'd conquer it.
Graham:	They've discovered a tumour in my thigh... in the muscle...
Mark:	He was to have a hind quarters amputation... a very rare and obviously unpleasant operation... but even then Graham found the opportunity for laughter.
Graham:	With no other blind amputees competing... I'll be sure to win the American Open!
Mark:	He was in hospital for five weeks...
Marie:	I wondered how we'd manage... but once he came home... we just got on with it. The hospital staff loved him, and were amazed by his immediate determination to walk.
Mark:	And walk he did... he didn't like to use his wheelchair and often chose to walk even though it hurt him. Soon, Marie was telling me about a near miss Graham had... with his specially designed artificial leg... adapted so that he could still play golf!
Marie:	We were at the Golf course practice ground. Graham'd got into the buggy and let his artificial leg drop on the floor... right onto the accelerator. He really took off down that hill... at the bottom was a ditch... he was well aware of that... but had no idea where the steering wheel was, so had no option but to roll himself out of the damned thing which sped its way down the hill towards the Practice Green.

GRAHAM - World's Fastest Blind Man!

	When I got to him, he was clutching his stomach... but he wasn't in any pain...
Graham:	I was just pissing myself laughing!
Mark:	Things seemed to be improving. Then, Graham phoned following his first holiday after the operation. "How was the holiday then?
Graham:	It was lovely... yeh...
Mark:	Something in his voice told me that was not the full story...
Graham:	We had to come home early.
Mark:	What happened?
Graham:	My other leg's started to swell up...
Mark:	It was so difficult to know what to say to this catalogue of problems Graham encountered. It was hard to empathise with such suffering. I have to admit that, sometimes, I postponed calls to Graham because I felt my responses were so inadequate. I believed that, as a friend, I should know what to say... the right words only emerged when we were together... and that was far less frequent now we'd moved away.
Graham:	The cancer's gone into my other leg... and they've found nodules in my lungs.
Mark:	Are they going to be able to do anything?
Graham:	They're not gonna do another amputation...
Mark:	Graham... how are you coping?
Graham:	It's difficult. They may do some chemo... but they're not sure I'll stand up to it.
Mark:	What do you want them to do?
Graham:	Anything... anything to give me a little extra time here with Marie.
Marie:	The doctor had told him it was terminal.
Mark:	Graham battled for another year. He died in October 1999.

Section 1

Marie: Graham was desperate to enjoy one more Christmas and to see in the millennium... it wasn't to be. Towards the end he was in terrible pain. He'd been fighting cancer for 47 years. He was simply too tired to go on.

Mark: A few weeks before he died he'd been playing football with our boys.
(Slides[5] of Graham with Mark, Marie, Ollie and Charlie.)
He had this special ball... which he bequeathed to them... with ball bearings inside so he could hear where the ball was. When he lost his leg he used to stand on his crutches and took shots at Ollie and Charlie with his other leg or his crutch. They were amazed at how often he scored! This time he was in his wheelchair... in pain... but he still played... throwing the ball for them and doing the occasional header. Graham still wanted to give... just as in 1982 he'd given hours and hours of his time doing interviews for *Race To Be Seen*.
Before I interviewed Graham's mum and dad, I remember them saying...

Maud & Harry: No one will be interested in our story!

Mark: They were wrong...

---

[5] These slides are available from MBA Literary Agents Ltd. See Footnote 2.

Section 2: Graham's Early Years

Maud:	Right from when our Graham was born we could see bloodlines through his eyes. Dr Bell at the clinic said:
All:	It's pressure... it'll go in six weeks.
Maud:	Then he had three nights of violent crying with this thick yellow discharge coming from both his eyes... nothing could pacify him. I took him to the clinic again.
All:	Mrs Salmon! It's only teething!
Maud:	*(To the Nurse)* When he's in his cot under the light... you can see something white at the back of his eye... one day I caught my Harry testing his sight with a card. *(To Harry.)* What are you doing?
Harry:	He can't see out of this eye. *(Referring to the right eye.)*
Maud:	Don't be daft. Course he can.
Harry:	He can't... look!
Maud:	He covered up the good eye and put this toy in front of Graham. He never followed it or nothing.
Harry:	We did it with the other eye and straight away he followed it.
Maud:	Finally, they gave me an appointment at Moorfields Eye Hospital. After two and a half hours being passed from doctor to doctor, I was introduced to Mr Mason... a senior consultant...
Mr Mason:	Mrs Salmon, there's something I have to say to you that I want you to understand.
Maud:	He put his arm around my shoulder.
Mr Mason:	I'm afraid Graham has a serious problem with his right eye.
Maud:	He was ever so kind.
Mr Mason:	It can't be cured.
Maud:	He seemed to understand how I was feeling.
Mr Mason:	We'll have to take his eye away...
Maud:	Do what?

Section 2

Mr Mason: We also need to check the other one. The white you can see in Graham's eye is a tumour...

Maud: A tumour?

Mark: She was told that unless they took his eye away, Graham would suffer a very unpleasant death with the tumour spreading to his brain.

Mr Mason: We need to do this operation as soon as possible. You'll need to bring him in at two o' clock on Monday, next week.

Maud: I don't know how I got home. It was shattering... just numb... it had all been so brutal.

SONG 2: **BREAKING LIVES** [6]

Mark: *How can you tell this torment to your husband*
When you haven't quite found the words to tell yourself?
How can you find the terms that won't destroy him
And speak them in tones that you can control yourself?
Breaking news... breaking dreams... breaking lives.
Where did she find the strength and the courage from?

Harry: I got home at lunchtime and there was no lunch. Maud and Graham weren't there. I told June, our seven year old, that she'd have to have sandwiches instead.
Maud returned at about twenty past one. She was crying when she told me.

Maud: He's got to go to hospital. They've got to take his eye out.

Harry: Do what?

Maud: Take his eye out.

Harry: What for?

Maud: He's got a tumour. I wanted you to be there Harry...
I didn't know what to say... we've got to take him on Monday afternoon and they're going to take his eye away.

Harry: Are you sure?

Maud: Of course I am!

---

[6] CDs of the songs from GRAHAM are available from dbda. See Footnote 1.

GRAHAM - World's Fastest Blind Man!

Harry:	Can't they do anything else?
Maud:	They told me they couldn't!
Harry:	I've been telling you for weeks that there's something wrong! But the clinic... you told me they thought you were making a fuss.
Maud:	I've been in that hospital for over four hours with Graham crying almost all the time... come back home and what do I get...
Harry:	It makes me so angry! *(Silence.)*
Maud:	It's not my fault... it's no use shouting! We've just got to get on with it.
Harry:	Maud, I'm... *(Silence.)*
Maud:	We wanted a photo of him, to remember what he looked like... before they did it. That was very important to us.
Harry:	First thing on Saturday morning we went to the photographers and booked an appointment for four o' clock that afternoon. *(Slide[7] of the original photograph.)*
Maud:	We was a bit disappointed... we couldn't line his eyes up proper... but it was a lovely photograph. It was a lovely photograph other than that. That was the only thing we sort of pointed out to one another. On Monday afternoon at 1.30 we arrived at Moorfields.
Harry:	At 3.30 we had to leave Graham there to have his operation... the Children's Ward was in quarantine with the Chicken pox epidemic.
Maud:	I felt as if the world had come to an end... I was crying so much that you bought me a clock... a smashing little mantle clock... lovely little thing. I remember in the shop I was all red eyed and everybody was staring... they probably thought we'd had an argument. When we went back after his operation we didn't know what to expect.

---

(7) These slides are available from MBA Literary Agents Ltd. See Footnote 2.

Section 2

Harry:	He had a pad over his right eye and his head was all bandaged up. They'd put cardboard sleeves down his arms to stop him clawing at the bandage.
Maud:	We were going up there every day for the next three weeks, weren't we? Nothing else in our lives seemed important. It still brings a lump to my throat to talk about it. On the third week they sent for you, didn't they? When he come back again I says to him... "What did they want?"
Harry:	They're are going to give him some radium.
Maud:	What for?
Harry:	They've found seeds in his other eye. They can kill the seeds with the radium.
Maud:	He was really upset... he punched the wall and Gawd knows what he didn't do.
Harry:	They said they couldn't promise anything.
Maud:	The next time I went, he hadn't got his bandages on and when we walked in he was sitting there, and.. it was a shock... to see him sitting there. His left eye was bloodshot from the radium... and he had no eyeball in the other one... just a socket there. It was a proper shock... it really upset me.
Harry:	We told Junie he'd had his eye taken out and he looked a bit different.
Maud:	We explained what a dolly looked like when it had lost one of its eyes and we said... "That's what our Graham looks like." She accepted it quite well really. They made him an artificial eye. I had to put it in and take it out. It was very unnerving at first... but I soon got the hang of it.
Harry:	He had ten lots of radium put in, spread over eighteen months.
Maud:	He'd go in for four or five days at a time, and when he came out his eye was black and blue and swollen, like he'd had a punch up.

GRAHAM - World's Fastest Blind Man!

Harry: They said it never hurt him... but it did...

Maud: He used to bury his head in the cushions on the armchair with his backside in the air rocking backwards and forwards listening to one record: *Rock Around the Clock*.

Harry: The fact we couldn't explain why it had to happen was probably the worst thing about it! We bought him lots of toys. We brought him this little piano. He just looked at it. That was it... he didn't want to know.

Maud: The sight in his eye was going gradually... he had to walk right up to the television and stare right into it... he used to shake it sometimes... shake the picture out of it.

Harry: After the final radium treatment I gets this telegram asking me to go to the hospital.

Maud: I don't know what I went for... they didn't want to know me!

Mark: Graham's father was told the treatment wasn't working... but they could offer a new and more finely tuned course of radiotherapy. His parents had to decide whether he should undergo this new "experimental" treatment. There were problems... even if his sight was saved, there was the possibility that his eyeball might shrink.

Maud: We'd 've done anything... anything to try and save his sight... what little he had.

SONG 2b: **BREAKING LIVES (Reprise)**

Mark: *Think of the homes you know in town or country*
And you'll see that this family here is just the same
Like you or me they share in normal living
But out of the blue this bolt breaks their pattern down.
Will their son now be scarred for the rest of his life...
or even die?
How will they face the problems the future holds?

Maud: It was a Friday. We had to be there at nine o' clock. We had to sit through the operation, like, wait until it was done. They wanted to tell us there and then whether it had been a success.

Section 2

Harry:	It was two or three hours... sitting there... waiting.
Maud:	Eventually Mr Mason came out...
Mr Mason:	I'm afraid, it's not good news.
Maud:	He was almost in tears himself poor man.
Mr Mason:	His eye just hasn't stood up to the treatment.
Harry:	What do you mean?
Mr Mason:	The only safe solution is to remove it.
Maud:	Couldn't we give him one of our eyes?
Mr Mason:	I wish it was as simple as that.
Maud:	But he'll be blind?
Mr Mason:	Yes, he will... but he'll have a future.
Harry:	What could we say? *(Mr Mason exits. Silence.)* I remember wondering whether he'd thank us for what we'd done...
Maud:	I thought the pain and suffering he'd been through might affect him.
Harry:	We had the opportunity to finish life for him. Were we just being selfish keeping him alive but letting him go blind?
Maud:	Totally blind.
Harry:	Our heads were, like, bursting with questions that no one could answer.
Maud:	What'll happen when he's an adult?
Harry:	Will he make friends?
Maud:	Will he ever find a wife?
Harry:	Will he ever find a job?
Maud:	We wondered how all our friends and relations would react?
Harry:	And how will we cope?
Maud:	We'd never even met a blind person before...
Harry:	... yet Graham was to be our responsibility.

GRAHAM - World's Fastest Blind Man!

Maud:	We had to prepare him for life.
Harry:	We were determined to succeed...
Maud:	But would determination be enough?
Harry:	Little did we know then how proud we'd become of our Graham.
Maud:	Little did we know then that cancer would strike again.
Harry:	At half past one he came out of the Theatre and was pushed into the lift.
Maud:	We weren't allowed to see him.
Harry:	They told us everything was "as well as could be expected".
Maud:	They said we should go home and phone in the evening. The next day we went up to Moorfields.
Harry:	We thought we could hear him laughing, didn't we?
Maud:	We went in there and he was playing with the Sister... large as life.
Harry:	I played with the motors on the floor with him, didn't I? He was really laughing.
Maud:	The first time we'd ever seen him happy, weren't it?
Harry:	He was a changed boy after that.
Mark:	His sister June remembers him as a baby...
June:	When Mum was in hospital having Susan, I had to put Graham's eyes in. To be quite honest, I was always frightened in case I hurt him. I didn't always put them in the right socket, or I'd put them in upside down. It'd be a bit awkward. I used to get in a bit of a panic... but *most* times I used to get them in alright!

Section 3: Being Blind as a Child

Mark: I was sent away to Boarding School at the age of nine... those first few months away from my mum and dad proved to be the most confusing and upsetting period in my life...
Graham went as a weekly boarder at the age of four!

(The following conversation occurs as Graham is taken from Maud to the RNIB school.)

Maud: I don't want him to go away!

RNIB Doctor: You don't want him tied to your apron strings all your life.

Mark: The RNIB obviously weren't going to agree!

RNIB Doctor: He needs to be independent.

Maud: I'll have you know we've always let him be as "independent" as possible.

RNIB Doctor: You're not equipped to teach him the things a blind person needs to know in order to be "independent".

Maud: He's only four!

RNIB Doctor: He'll come home at weekends.

Maud: I don't want him to go away!

Mark: Nevertheless, arrangements were made and Graham was enrolled at the Sunshine Home for the blind.

Graham: Some of the children there were educationally sub-normal and very destructive... I found their behaviour difficult to understand.

Junie: Mum and dad were very upset, very upset... sort of... really on thorns all the time. "Is he alright?" and, "Would they look after him properly... keep him clean?"

Graham: I used to look forward to going home at the weekends... I'd come straight home and put my favourite record on. *(Rock Around The Clock.)*

Maud: He used to dance a lot with Junie. If he couldn't get his own way he used to be wicked to her... he used to pull her hair. She was good to him though... she'd do anything he wanted.

GRAHAM - World's Fastest Blind Man!

Junie: At the weekends when Graham was home it was all Graham, Graham, Graham. Me and Susan were forgotten. They were so wrapped up in him that, to be honest, there were times when I hated him. I look back and think how silly I was, but at the time I hated him.

Mark: Something that I've always found amazing is that Graham has no memory of ever seeing anything... not even light and dark... so the concept of seeing doesn't exist for him... The way I've always explained what a blind person "sees", and Graham seemed to approve of it, is to say what does your knee see? Nothing. So, how does someone who's blind experience their environment? Graham uses what he calls Sound Shadows.

Graham: They're echoes I hear from objects... the bigger the object the better. In quiet surroundings I can detect lamp-posts and trees... sounds quite impressive until I tell you that it's never early enough to stop myself from getting a bloody big bruise off them though!
Various factors affect how well these sound shadows work... a strong wind can destroy any hope of hearing them... a pneumatic drill makes me lose my sense of direction almost completely; you could say then that I "feel" blind. Nothing was real to me until I'd touched it. That posed a problem... not everything I wanted to feel was easily examined by a small boy.
One example, is something that sighted people take for granted... light. The best way for me to experience it was to touch it... so with the kind of precision demonstrated by the Dam busters *(Perhaps here the Dam busters music could be used and all, as aeroplanes, get into position!)*, Susan took me into our narrow hallway and lined me up underneath the lampshade hanging from the ceiling. There was little point in me touching it unless it was switched on... so...

Susan: I clicked the switch... and he was off!

Graham: With one foot on the wall I inched my way up towards the ceiling until I could feel the warmth of the bulb on my face...

Section 3

Susan:	...then, like Columbus landing on America, he touched the "light".
Graham:	Owwwww!
Susan:	The joy of discovery was tempered by pain...
Graham:	...not just from the bulb!
Maud:	His shoes had been muddy... *(Maud smacks his backside)* ...my walls had been very clean.
Graham:	*(Holding his backside.)* ... and my path to en"light"enment had to lie low for a few days while mum cleaned up my quest for illumination!
Maud:	His toys gave him some idea of what things looked like.
Graham:	I had loads of soldiers... they all had names. I could usually find something different about each of them: how they were standing, the guns they were holding or the shape of their uniforms... but the Arab soldiers were a bit misleading... their thick robes left me with the impression that all Arabs are extremely fat!
Harry:	He had a stamp book and stamps...
Susan:	I don't know why. He couldn't have known what the bloody hell they looked like!
Graham:	I got mum and dad to buy me a bike... *(The cast make a bike.)*
Maud:	First... a three-wheeler...
Harry:	... then, when his knees were knocking on top of it we bought him a two-wheeler. *(The bike transforms into an exciting looking "monster" two wheeler.)*
Maud:	... and put stabilisers on it.
Harry:	He used to go up and down the street and never went off the kerb.
Graham:	*(Proudly)* One day I ran someone over...
Man:	You little bugger... why don't you bloody look where you're going!

GRAHAM - World's Fastest Blind Man!

Graham: I'm blind... You should get out of my way!!!

Man: I was so bloody shocked that I phoned the newspaper up.

Graham: And they came down and took some pictures... of me! *(Newspaper pictures of Graham on the trike.)* [8]

Maud: I can only remember one time when a sighted kid took advantage of his blindness.

John: Oy... come here you... feel this.

Graham: He had this piece of wood... as I touched it, he placed his hand over mine and pressed it onto a nail sticking up out of it. It really hurt!

Maud: The boy's mother was furious!

Mother: *(Running onto stage in comic manner!)* You wait till I get you, you little sod!!! *(Chases him off stage!)*

Graham: The 'little sod' was always really friendly after that!

Mark: It's not only children who have the propensity for cruelty... Graham once told me of a man who had just bought some second hand hi-fi equipment from him... real top of the range stuff. Shortly after the buyer had disappeared into the mist, Graham discovered that he had been paid in ten pound notes... and not twenty's.

Harry: Sometimes he used it to his advantage. Many's the time we used to think he was asleep, but unbeknown to us... he had these bloody Braille reading books underneath the sheets... he was supposed to be sleeping!

Mark: On his first visit to our new house, he went into our bathroom and locked the door... I could hear him fumbling about and I then saw from under the door that he had not switched the light on. I was thinking it would be more difficult for him to find the unusually situated pull switch because he was blind... so... went through an elaborate description from the other side of the door as to how he should find it. He obediently switched the light on and said:

Graham: I still can't see the bloody toilet!

---

(8) These slides are available from MBA Literary Agents Ltd. See Footnote 2.

Section 3

Maud:	One Friday he told us he wanted a white stick.
Harry:	So we got him one... a special one for children...
Graham:	Can I go out?
Maud:	Just to the sweet shop.
Graham:	Can I have some money?
Maud:	*(Handing Graham the money.)* Susan!
Graham:	Why are you calling her?
Maud:	To look after you.
Graham:	I want to go on my own.
Maud:	No!
Graham:	Why not?
Maud:	You're not used to it yet... now if you want those sweets you'd...
Graham:	Alright then!
Maud:	I went back into the kitchen but was soon joined by Susan... puffing and panting.
Susan:	Graham wouldn't let me go with him!
Maud:	I had a fit... I went out there and he was nowhere to be seen.
Graham:	I was at the sweet shop!
Maud:	They'd given him free sweets and were chatting away to him. After that we let him go out on his own.
Graham:	Shortly after... an old lady stopped me... she was a bit like one of those Harry Enfield caricatures!
Woman:	Oy you!
Graham:	Who me?
Woman:	You're a wicked little boy!
Graham:	Me?
Woman:	You shouldn't pretend to be blind!

GRAHAM - World's Fastest Blind Man!

Graham:	I am blind!
Woman:	You don't think I believe that, do you!
Graham:	Come and ask my mum if you want!
Woman:	It's not funny being blind you know!
Graham:	It is sometimes!
Woman:	Cheeky little bleeder! *(She walks out.)*
Graham:	Stupid cow!
Mark:	The condemned houses in Woodland Street, where the young Graham Salmon lived, became a magnificent playground for him and Susan to explore...
Susan:	Once, with one of my friends, we got into this derelict factory by the side of the railway station in Dalston.
Madge:	Go on Graham... I dare you to climb onto that beam.
Graham:	Easy!
Madge:	Go on then.
Susan:	Go on... show her what you can do!
Graham:	I climbed up a pillar and pulled myself onto the beam.
Madge:	He's amazing your brother is, isn't he?
Susan:	He can do anything!
Graham:	Instinctively, I played up to this encouragement. *(Does some funny "party tricks".)*
Madge:	Wow! Amazing!
Susan:	Graham... what are you doing?
Madge:	Cor... he's so clever!
Graham:	*(As he gets to his feet.)* My tightrope act!
Susan:	Don't! You're being stupid.
Madge:	No let him...
Susan:	No... he'll hurt himself... Get down now, else I'm telling mum!

Section 3

Graham:	I took a few cautious steps... then, crouched down and crawled a little further...
Susan:	Are you alright... Graham?
Graham:	It was narrow and covered with dust, which made it seem slippery.
Susan:	You stay here Madge... I'll go and get mum...
Graham:	I was frightened!
Madge:	Susan!
Graham:	I was petrified!
Madge:	Just stay still... Susan'll be back in a minute.
Graham:	I really thought I was going to faint!
Maud:	Graham! What on earth 're you doing?
Graham:	I could barely speak...
Maud:	I wasn't quite so dumbstruck!
Graham:	I won't do it again Mum... honest!
Maud:	He didn't...
Mark:	But his spirit wasn't dampened...
Maud:	... no... not in the slightest!
Graham:	From the very beginning, I could sense that I was "special". Being "normal" was never a consideration - I wanted to be the best!

Section 4: A World Record

Mark: Defining... moments... can you identify yours?
(The cast act out the scenes as they are described.)
One of mine was discovering the magic of Theatre... through going to see David Bowie, on his massive 1973 Aladdin Sane tour, live at the Colston Hall in Bristol. His band, The Spiders from Mars came on, that in itself was amazing, having only seen them rarely as icons on TV before... then suddenly my hero was there in person... I couldn't figure out where he'd come from or how he'd got there... looking back, I realise it was only a very simple lighting effect... but pure magic in the eyes of this fifteen year old schoolboy. The next day I failed my French exam as I spent the whole time dreaming of that fantastic evening... Graham was clear about his defining moment... picture this... *(The scene is set by the cast playing the various items as it is described)* a domestic scene... a boy... Graham and his Uncle... just finished a game of cricket in the garden... washing at the sink... his Uncle approaches with a book... a big book... **The Guinness Book of Records**...

Claude: *(Holding the book.)* Listen to this Graham.

Graham: *(Washing his hands.)* My uncle couldn't have known... as he dropped this tit-bit in my ear... he was loading my gun.

Claude: "The fastest time recorded by a blind man running 100 yards is eleven seconds by Geoff Bull, aged 19 of Chippenham, Wiltshire, in a race at Worcester College for the blind on 26th October 1954".

Graham: My target from that moment on was to have my name in **The Guinness Book of Records** as the worlds' fastest blind runner.

Claude: I had no idea that he'd set out to actually do this... he was too busy being a rock star... playing his guitar and writing songs...

Graham: I'd been the first person in the school to get a twelve-string guitar... I was so proud of it and my group, the Agreeables...

Mark: ... renamed The Disagreeables by his father

Claude: ... for obvious reasons.

Graham: We burst onto the school music scene like the **Stones** in

Section 4

	miniature. One of our gigs was stopped because a group of girls were screaming so hysterically at us.
Mark:	Their Head teacher did not approve!
Headteacher:	You boys should stop your rock star dreams and concentrate on something that will get you on in life... doing your work!
Graham:	We knew we were destined for stardom... so we ignored him... and went on to do an amazing recording session at Decca. *(Play extract from Decca recording together with slide of the Agreeables.)*[(9)]
Mark:	Some of his friends were not so complimentary suggesting Graham had Van Gough's ear for music!
Graham:	This was a very special time... music, friends and sport... what more could a lad want?
Mark:	The Pop career was somewhat short lived but under the guidance of his inspirational teacher, Bill Aitken, Graham began to develop a deeper interest in athletics. Bill spotted his potential and spent time with him training.
Graham:	He staged a race where I took on everyone in the school... blind and partially sighted.
Mark:	Graham won...
Graham:	Easily! The world record now seemed a very real possibility...
Mark:	Bill organised an unsuccessful attempt...
Graham:	... but there'd be other opportunities.
Mark:	Three days before his 26th birthday, Graham Salmon broke the World Record for a Blind runner... running the 100 metres in 11.4 seconds...
Graham:	... and my name duly appeared in *The Guinness Book of Records*.
Mark:	But how does a blind person do the hundred metres?

---

(9) CDs of this and the other songs are available from dbda. See Footnote 1.
Slides are available from MBA Literary Agents Ltd. See Footnote 2.

GRAHAM - World's Fastest Blind Man!

Graham: Two callers stand on the track, one at 30 metres so that their voice is clear as I leave the blocks. The other, stands just beyond the finish, and takes over as the first moves out of my path.

Each, call continuously using a number system. Five, the centre track number, means I'm straight. If the number gets lower I'd know that I'm running slightly towards the inside of the track... likewise higher towards the outside. The more the numbers change the more I know I've deviated so if I hear the caller calling out 1... I'd know I'm about to be speared by a javelin!

Mark: We did a lot of blindfold work with 17-year-old Matthew Allen, who was playing Graham in the original *Race To Be Seen*. Matt, who has gone on to become a successful professional actor and director, spent the first two days on a residential drama course in a blindfold. He did complete blindfold rehearsals of the play providing the cast with lots of scope for practical jokes... but never had an accident...

Graham: Not until he did some running.

Mark: He was becoming quite confident about that...

Graham: I challenged him to a time trial.

Mark: We were all interested to see how he'd fare. Marie went to the 100 metre mark to do the final sixty metres call.

Graham: Matt was determined to get a respectable time.

Mark: He set off at full tilt...

Graham: But the caller at 30 metres had never called before...
I heard him go... 5... 6... 7...8... 9... 10... 11... he was just like counting...

Mark: Matt kept on adjusting himself more in the wrong direction and, still running full tilt, he ran straight into a fence with a metal bar at thigh level. The caller didn't say stop... I'll never know why. I'd set him up to do it... I was responsible... it was really horrific... but when I looked over at Graham he was wetting himself with laughter!

Graham: Matt learnt more about being blind from that experience than anything I could say or do.

Section 5: Marie

Mark: Meanwhile, back in his final week of Secondary School, Graham found his (metaphorical) eye had been taken by one of the young matrons... his school friend, Pete Young was determined to get them together...

Pete: Marie Pegg fancies you mate.

Graham: How do you know?

Pete: You can tell.

Graham: How?

Pete: She's always faking occasions to meet you.

Graham: Leave it out Pete... you're winding me up!

Pete: She is... and she's always setting you up as an example to everyone else mate.

Graham: Rubbish!

Pete: ... about how good your posture is. She does... she fancies you!

Graham: Are you sure?

Pete: She thinks you're the King!

Graham: He just made me start thinking about her more than I would have done otherwise...

Pete: Well, what do you think?

Graham: I'll see what she says.

Pete: Let me know, won't you?

Graham: Course I will.
I knew she'd be going up to change the beds at about 6:45. The sports news came on then, so I deliberately left my radio in the dormitory... at twenty to seven I went up. *(Marie is making the beds. Graham moves towards his radio and in so doing bumps into her.)*

Marie: You made me jump... what are you doing up here?

Graham: My radio's up here... come to hear the sports news.
I did feel a bit daring... there was a silence for what seemed like ages.

GRAHAM - World's Fastest Blind Man!

Marie: I didn't help... I was quite shy of fellahs...

Graham: In the end I just went ahead, and asked... well, it wasn't going to be a lifetime commitment!

Marie: I knew he was going to ask me out cos Pete Young had told me at breakfast time, so I'd already made my mind up... "That'd be really nice."

Graham: Are you free this week, or do you want to wait until I've left, then, maybe we could go to the pictures or something.

Marie: I'm free on Tuesday. Why don't we go to Hyde Park?

Graham: Yeah.

Mark: And so, the story goes... they had their first kiss... and who should walk in... but Pete Young...

Pete: What are you doing Graham?

Graham: I... I dropped a book... Marie was up here, so... so I asked her to help me look for it.

Pete: I reckon you were feeling more than a Braille book there Graham!

Graham: That summer with Marie was wonderful.

Section 6: King of the College

Mark: The following September Graham started at Worcester College for the blind.

Graham: I needed Maths to qualify for the RNIB's computer programming course. I wanted to do the course in a year and leave.

Mark: But the college demanded that he stay for two years and do A' levels as well.

Graham: I was never committed to them. In the words of my History teacher:

Teacher: Graham has made little effort to reduce his extensive ignorance!

Graham: There was little to enthuse me about sharing the next two years with eighty blind boys... I missed Marie, and that made it even more difficult to settle.

Marie: I went to see him every other weekend... wasn't allowed inside the College... even if it was raining... they just said:

Teacher: He won't be long.

Marie: They couldn't handle it.

Graham: I had a photograph of Marie by my bed. It made her feel closer.

Mark: What eventually helped him to settle was his other love... horse racing.

Graham: Each race is like a puzzle to be solved... and the winnings a reward when I get it right.

Mark: Graham was always a gambler...

Graham: Not always... I didn't start till I was eleven!

Mark: He always came out with a profit at the end of the year...

Marie: *(Disagreeing.)* Huh!

Mark: ... at least that's what he told me.
On the occasions we went to a Casino, Lady Luck always looked on him favourably... though he'd claim it was skill:

Graham: I can tell where the ball's going to land by the sound of it spinning!

Mark: If it wasn't true, it was certainly uncanny!

GRAHAM - World's Fastest Blind Man!

Graham:	Racing was a subject on which I could talk with authority... my first tip paid for a glorious pub crawl... I was soon the driving force behind the racing fraternity at the College!
Mark:	But that was only the beginning of the story... Graham wrote a song for *Race*, music and lyrics, to tell of his expulsion... it's all absolutely true with nothing added for effect... apart from a few shoobie-doos!
SONG 3:	**KING OF THE COLLEGE**
	(All the cast should enter for this song and add shoobie-doos in the appropriate places. Where possible they should act out - using an imaginative array of body-props, etc - the events being described in the song.)
Graham:	***I was King of the College in my school day*** ***I organised the gambling to make it pay.*** ***A turf accountant paid me ten per cent commission*** ***And I ran my own book on the chart positions.***
	I'd meet with my friends in the library ***Study the form and pick a horse or three*** ***For a year I took bets and avoided detection***
Mark:	***He even won money on the General Election.***
Graham:	***Until the History teacher came snooping around.*** ***He caught me laying money with a bookie in town-*** ***he said:***
Teacher:	***"Gambling at your age is against the law!"***
Mark:	***He cancelled the bet...***
Graham:	***... and the horse came in at nine to four!***
	I was taken to the head and was promptly sent home...
All:	***The King of the College was kicked off his throne!***
Mark:	***But the send off they gave him made the teachers frown***
Graham:	***And the bookie sent the money on... once all the fuss*** ***had died down!***
	(Repeat Verse 1.)
Graham:	My History teacher, who was responsible for that damming school report, not only caught me placing the bet, but was alone, on breakfast duty, on the morning of my departure.
Teacher:	When it came to the announcements, the cheeky blighter stood up:
Graham:	As you will be aware, I am leaving today, but I have one

Section 6

	parting thought which I'd like you all to bear in mind.
Teacher:	I tried to get him to sit down! *(Makes his way over to Graham.)*
Graham:	Remember my friends...
Teacher:	Sit down boy... sit down! *(Tries to get him to sit down.)*
Graham:	"Radix malum est cupidas".
Mark:	Roughly translates as "Money is the root of all evil".
Teacher:	*(To Mark.)* You can shut up too!
Graham:	Mr Downes was not amused... and, as I sat down, the entire dining room erupted into a rousing chorus of "*For He's a Jolly Good Fellow*" accompanied by clapping, stamping and lots of banging on tables. One of the kitchen maids came out of the kitchen and kissed me goodbye, wishing me luck. She said they'd all miss me!
Maud:	The headmaster...
Mark:	... who was also a Justice of the Peace...
Maud:	... he rang up and told us that Graham was to be sent home.
Harry:	I wasn't at all bothered...
June:	That's not true! You said... "The little sod! I'll have a go at him when he gets home."
Harry:	I could hardly let on to a JP that I knew all about it!
June:	No... dad. You'd bought this expensive blue trunk for all his gear to go in... you were saying: "All that bloody money we've spent out and he's not been there long!"
Maud:	There was twelve of them that got suspended. He used to take bets off some of the teachers, but of course he couldn't say anything or he'd have got them into real trouble.
Mark:	And what was Graham's reaction... ashamed... worried... concerned?
Graham:	No way!!! I was delighted to be awarded an extra fortnight's holiday!

(To link this section with the next, the cast circle around - as though on the dodgems - perhaps fairground music could play.)

Section 7: Unemployment - Employment

Mark: Sometimes Graham made his blindness appear as a bonus... an additional ability... ordinary events all too often became extraordinary... dodgem cars being one example... his driving was, you could say, a sight for sore eyes... the attendants having no choice but to allow him to contravene the "one way only" rule!!!
But how did he feel inside? Was he always able to be so positive? He was once asked in a TV interview if he'd ever been bitter about being blind... he said no... then the interviewer probed further... there was a slight pause for thought and then Graham replied:

Graham: Once. After I'd became a fully qualified computer programmer but still no one would give me a job.

Maud: He wrote about sixty letters of application in one go... and this was in the days when there were no word processors. He got four replies.

Graham: I'd get my guitar out and write songs about the injustices of the world or lie on my bed and just cry. I'd virtually no money... so I couldn't go out and do anything either. Most days I'd lie in bed till mid-morning. In the afternoon I'd stroll along to the local bookies, listen to a few races on the exchange telegraph broadcast, and bet with an average stake of 20p. If I won, I'd buy me and mum a jam doughnut.

Mark: It was around that time that, what Graham describes as one of the most "chilling episodes" of his life occurred.

Graham: It was a quiet afternoon, and I was out walking, when suddenly I heard the sound of screeching tyres and a loud thud. The car accelerated again... and flashed past me. A hit and run accident. I was the only witness!
A crowd of people soon gathered around. A woman was crying... it was her son... she said he was only ten years old... he was making no noise.

Bystander: I think his arm's broken. Has someone phoned for an ambulance?

Graham: They were saying that nobody had "seen" the accident. I carried on walking. Should I have done more... stood in the road, thrown something? I felt sick... I'd been so useless. That memory has haunted me ever since.

Section 7

Mark:	Four months later... Graham was still without a job.
Graham:	I thought I might stand more chance if I did audio typing... I could type so I couldn't foresee any major problems... I phoned the RNIB to get their advice.
Employment Officer:	You'll need to be trained!
Graham:	I can already type!
E. O.:	You have to be trained at our college.
Graham:	I've already done the RNIB's computer programming course.
E. O.:	This is different.
Graham:	What do I have to do?
E. O.:	It's a two-year course. Shall I put you on the waiting list?
Graham:	I can start now!
E. O.:	There's a three-year waiting list.
Graham:	What about telephony?
E. O.:	Now, this course lasts for... let me see... I think it's ten... no eleven weeks...
Graham:	Excellent...
E. O.:	There's a waiting list for that too... it'll be ten months before...
Graham:	*(Graham slams the phone down.)* I don't believe this!
E. O.:	Mr Salmon? Mr Salmon? Well, how very rude. He's slammed the phone down on me without so much as a by your leave! You try and help... what do you get back? Some folk will never be satisfied!
Graham:	I wasn't going to wait for the RNIB... so, with mum reading articles from newspapers and books onto tapes, I practised audio typing at home and applied for jobs advertised in the evening papers.

(Personnel Officers animate the scene by an abstract physical presentation highlighting the prejudicial views they represent. They repeat their lines crescending to a shout, whereupon Graham slams the phone down. A note to directors would be to <u>avoid</u> [like the plague] the PO's merely circling Graham. The should be portrayed as exaggeratedly patronising.)

GRAHAM - World's Fastest Blind Man!

Officer 1:	It could be a bit difficult... }
Officer 2:	You wouldn't be able to manage... }
Officer 3:	We're not able to employ blind people... }
	(Silence.)
Officers 1 - 3:	Don't worry Mr Salmon... we will call you back.
Graham:	People'd be interested... I'd say "I'm blind." and they'd lose interest.
Officer 1:	Oh... oh dear...
Officer 2:	Oh dear, oh dear!
Officer 3:	Oh dear, oh dear, oh dear!
Officer 1:	Oh dear... oh... oh, I'm afraid that could be a bit difficult.
Graham:	Why's that then?
Officer 2:	Erm... well... the office entrance is down a small side turning. Big lorries are often going in and out.
Officer 3:	A blind person would be a severe drain on our sophisticated system.
Officer 1:	The staff aren't very thoughtful...
Officer 2:	... the toilet seats are sometimes dirty.
Officer 3:	We make tea for meetings... and we... erm... we take it in turns...
Officers 1 - 3:	You wouldn't cope.
Officer 3:	We're not able to employ blind people.
Officers 1 - 3:	It's a pity... we would... we would really like to have helped. *(Officers 2 & 3 exit.)*
Officer 1:	Oh... I am sorry... but... we're on the sixth floor... you won't be able to manage the stairs.
Graham:	What's wrong with them?
Officer 1:	They're... they're awkward... and... as I said... we're on the sixth floor.
Graham:	I said I was blind... not a bloody cripple! *(Silence.)*
Officer 1:	Perhaps I should take your number and call you back. *(They replace their respective receivers.)*

Section 7

Graham:	Montague Evans and Son did phone back and gave me the break I'd been looking for. Ironically the job I was offered was on the third floor... and you'll never guess what... there was a lift!
Mark:	Graham went on to have a highly successful career, twenty-five years of which were spent at the Abbey National. Most customers didn't realise he was blind... but there was one...
Client:	I have a query on my income tax and I'd like some advice.
Graham:	Could I have a look at your passbooks?
Client:	Of course.
Graham:	I'm just going inside to get some information... I won't keep you a minute.
Client:	Can't you read them out here? Is something wrong with your eyes?
Graham:	Yes... I'm blind.
Client:	Then get the Manager.
Graham:	Sorry, he's out today.
Client:	I'll see his deputy! You're not taking my books away.
Graham:	I only need them for a minute... to get some information from them.
Client:	You've said that twice already. I'm not unsympathetic, but I want to be served by someone who can see.
Graham:	I wanted to tell him that it was people like him who stopped people like me from getting jobs... and when we have those jobs, people like him stop us from getting on. I wanted to have a go at him... but I came in and asked Marion, our principal clerk, to see him.
Marion:	Then, as the client was on his way out, he had the cheek to say:
Client:	I suppose it's very generous of the company to give someone like that a job...
Mark:	Customers like that were few and far between.
Graham:	... and my time at the Abbey was very important to me...

GRAHAM - World's Fastest Blind Man!

Mark: The Abbey National gave Graham respect and recognition of his ability... not his disability. He was there because he was an asset to the company.

Jim: The watershed of his career came in the late 1980s... with the Financial Services Act and increased computerisation.

Mark: Finally an opportunity to do what he'd originally trained to do...

All: You won't be able to do it Graham...

Mark: Chorused a number of his colleagues...

Jim: ... who should have known Graham better...

Mark: It was like a red rag to a bull...

Graham: I hate being told that I can't do something... I'll set out to prove them wrong, or establish for myself that I can't do it... but I will not accept someone else making that decision for me.

Jim: With help from his reader, Graham became professionally qualified as a Financial Adviser and mastered the new computer system.

Mark: He soon faced the new challenge of creating his own personal customer base in a new flagship branch in the City...

Jim: Within two years he was the number one Financial Advisor in the City.

Mark: All these achievements led to an award in 1995 as one of RADAR's People of the Year award.

Jim: Graham Salmon MBE was an all round good guy... he had a major influence on the lives of his working colleagues throughout his twenty-five years at the Abbey... the amazing thing is... that he still does.

Mark: When I interviewed his colleagues back in 1982, they all had stories to tell about him...

Susie: There was the time that Rita lent him some records once and wrote on the bag...

All: "Thanks Graham... you were wonderful!"

Section 7

Susie:	... with three kisses printed underneath.
Marion:	We could just imagine him sitting on the train, completely unaware, displaying it to everyone
Marion & Susie:	... all the way home.
Marion:	Apparently some of the lads put the toilet brush upside down in the urinal with the bristly bits sticking out.
Susie:	When it touched his willy, he thought it was a rat and he jumped back in horror.
Graham:	But the funniest thing was that the people who had perpetrated that joke hid behind the door and switched the light off... so that I couldn't see them!!!

Section 8: Athletics

Mark:	So, back in 1972, Graham got his first job and at last some money. He began to see his friends from school again and they joined a sports club for the blind.
Graham:	But I wasn't happy with their organisation.
Marie:	Why don't you form your own?
Mark:	This set him thinking...
Marie:	The reception you got at the AGM proves you can't change it.
Graham:	I suppose you're right.
Mark:	Graham was concerned that he may upset some of the older members...
Marie:	... you mustn't let that worry you!
Graham:	We didn't, and formed our own club in 1973...
Marie:	... the same year as Graham and I were married.
Mark:	I know this breaks the conventions of a play... halting its progress and all that... but, this play does not do Marie justice. The words in the script are taken from interviews with the people involved in Graham's life... and Marie doesn't like doing interviews. So, instead I'll say my piece. Marie went out of her way to enable Graham to have, and moreover, enjoy the success he achieved. Always at his side, she never allowed herself to become sidelined... she accompanied him on his sporting journeys and became an important part on the management side of the British Blind Athletics team. She was always a devoted wife and throughout his final months an incomparable carer. I remember at Graham's funeral the priest said: "We are passing Graham's body into the care of God." .... and quite spontaneously... I thought... "God's got a hell of a job to live up to the care that Marie had given him." A few months after Graham's death, my wife was taken seriously ill... with breast cancer... we were really struggling... Marie took the initiative and came to look after our children and enabled Rachel to make a recovery. I don't know what would have happened if Marie hadn't helped out. It doesn't bear thinking about. Marie lives to "give".

Section 8

In his final months Graham wrote a number of songs and recorded them in his own recording studio... one was called simply... *My Wife*. I hope Graham's (performance of his) very personal song goes some way towards redressing the balance.

SONG 4: **"MY WIFE" BY GRAHAM SALMON** [10]

Graham:
(Actor or the pre-recorded original)

I have climbed many mountains reached many goals
And she's always been there beside me
She reaches out her hand and she touches my soul
And she gives all her love to guide me.

Always there behind the scenes
Never wanting the glory
Hope she knows how much she means...
Without her there's no story
Oh life... life is my wife

We have laughed in the sunshine and we've cried in the rain
And we've been through it all together
With a smile on our faces we can beat any pain
And we'll hold on to each other forever.

All:
Always there behind the scenes
Never wanting the glory
Hope she knows how much she means...
Without her there's no story
Oh life... life is my wife.

Mark:
(Cast form a straight line as though to dive into a pool)
The Club Graham and his friends formed... the Metropolitan Sports and Social Club for the Visually Handicapped...

Marie: Thankfully shortened to Metro.

Mark: ... was accorded charity status and Graham involved himself in the fundraising activities, participating in, amongst other things, a sponsored swim. Graham's swimming bore little relation to his fishy surname... Doggy Paddle was Graham's aquatic party piece!
(All dive in and do about eight strokes.)

---

[10] CDs of this and the other songs are available from dbda. See Footnote 1.

GRAHAM - World's Fastest Blind Man!

Marie:	*(As Marie speaks Graham kneels up and does a frantic doggy paddle!)* Even so, no one could talk him into doing any less than the others.
Mark:	His companions describe how they waited around for what seemed like weeks while he completed his thirty lengths!
Graham:	*(Graham pauses... his doggy paddle starts again... puts his arm out to touch the side of the pool.)* One! One of Metro's main ideas was to explore other sports so we sent a team to the Stoke Mandeville British Sports Association for the Disabled Athletics Championships.
Marie:	To our astonishment their running track was a strip of tarmac...
Graham:	... with a rose garden at the end...
Marie:	... hardly suitable for an athletics meeting...
Graham:	... even less so for blind competitors! We were expected, even in the straight line of a one hundred metres race, to team up with a sighted guide.
Marie:	Graham's couldn't keep up with him...
Graham:	... so I let go of his arm and charged for the line unaccompanied...
Marie:	I re-positioned myself at the end of Graham's lane and started calling...
Graham:	It was an amazing victory!
Marie:	... everyone was clapping...
Mark:	... but... because he finished without his guide...
Graham:	I was disqualified!
Mark:	Graham became even more determined to qualify for the Para-Olympics...
Graham:	However, selection was based on financial considerations, not athletic prowess.
Marie:	We were furious...
Mark:	They drew the Sports Council into the controversy... and

Section 8

	although the principle of selection was firmly established for the future...
Graham:	... there was no reversing the decisions already made.
Marie:	Graham was undeterred.
Mark:	Training three nights a week with Metro, they went on to stage their own National Athletics Championships using top officials.
Marie:	We really showed the Stoke Mandeville organisers how it should be done.
Graham:	One of the most frustrating aspects of being blind is the need to rely on others for help. I wanted to train every day, but didn't know of anyone who could fit in with those plans.
Marie:	He practised sprinting nightly...
Graham:	Marie would call me from the top of this steep hill, to test my strength and stamina.
Marie:	I didn't drive then so it was hard work... we were both knackered with the effort of it all but I wouldn't have had it any different.
Mark:	Graham became determined to find a professional coach to help him further his ambitions.
Graham:	For a full three years nobody seemed able to offer me much hope...
Mark:	He was even prepared to swap sports and contacted a High Jump coach...
Marie:	He phoned Ron Murray...
Graham:	... a real long shot...
Ron:	Hello... Ron Murray.
Marie:	Ron wasn't just any old coach.
Graham:	Hello... my name's Graham Salmon.
Marie:	*(Aside to the audience.)* He was <u>the</u> top High Jump coach.
Graham:	I'm looking for somebody to coach me for the high jump.
Marie:	*(Aside to the audience.)* Ron had just coached Barbara Inkpen to a silver medal at the Munich Olympics.

GRAHAM - World's Fastest Blind Man!

Graham:	I think I ought to tell you that I'm blind.
Ron:	Why the high jump? Recreation?
Graham:	No, I want to break the world record!
Ron:	Good for you sonny! I have helped blind people before.
Graham:	I later learnt that he had served as an officer in the Royal Navy and he sounded like one as he barked his instructions.
Ron:	Have to take a look at you... Monday evening, six o'clock... restaurant... Crystal Palace.
Graham:	He had this idea about how to teach me the fosberry flop!
Ron:	Girls... form a curve to show Graham the fosberry flop run in. *(To Graham.)* Now laddy... feel your way round the curve... and when you get to the biggest girl - jump!!!
Graham:	The idea didn't work... but it was an experience I certainly enjoyed!
Mark:	*(Slide of Graham doing the high jump* [11]*)* I've seen Graham doing the Fosberry flop successfully and I've seen him misjudge the moment when he should jump, landing across the bar, or missing the protected landing area altogether... there were no words of complaint... he'd get up and try again. He went on to set a new British high jump record for the totally blind at 1 metre 38... about neck height to an average adult.
Graham:	During one training session Ron was watching me running and suggested I took up sprinting.
Mark:	The following year Graham broke the 100 metres world record for a blind person...
Marie:	... and won the Kraft Daily Mail Athlete of the Month Award.
Graham:	Daley Thompson and Steve Ovett had been recent winners.
Ron:	Alan Wells was the runner up.
Graham:	I'd finally beaten an Olympic Champion!

(11) These slides are available from MBA Literary Agents Ltd. See Footnote 2.

Section 9: Race to be Seen - Epping Youth Theatre

Mark:	By 1982 Graham was a well established athlete... and I arrive in the story... on the phone as usual... Hello... could I speak to Graham Salmon please?
Marie:	Yes, hold on... I'll just fetch him.
Mark:	So this was the right number... the number of a man who, I'd been told, was blind and did some running.
Graham:	Hello...
Mark:	Hello... you won't know me... my name's Mark Wheeller. I'm phoning with what you'll probably consider to be a rather odd proposition... is it convenient to speak to you now?
Graham:	Mark's voice seemed friendly and sincere. Yes... go on...
Mark:	I've heard that you do some running... and... well, I'm the Director of the Epping Youth Theatre and we're involved in a project where we'd like... to write a play about someone who's overcome a disability...
Graham:	It sounds very interesting... but... well I'm very busy... I'm in training for The European Championships in Bulgaria.
Mark:	Wow! Sorry, I didn't realise... obviously I wouldn't expect you to make any kind of commitment over the phone and we'd need to know more about you before we could commit ourselves to the project... but I would like the opportunity to meet you if that's possible.
Graham:	My ego took over. We fixed a meeting for the end of the week.
Mark:	I was really excited... but would this "bloke who did some running" be a good subject... I knew nothing about him... and what would he think about us... a mere Youth Theatre?
Marie:	Who was that then?
Graham:	I was grinning broadly as I told Marie of Mark's ideas.
Marie:	A play?
Graham:	Yeh.
Marie:	*(Joking.)* I hope you told him where to go!
Graham:	It'll probably come to nothing.
Marie:	Graham!

GRAHAM - World's Fastest Blind Man!

Graham:	When Mark was late I wondered whether he was a crank, having a joke at my expense.
Mark:	The truth was that I'd got lost... I was three quarters of an hour late and really annoyed with myself. It was pouring with rain and at that time I only had a motorbike... *(It might be an idea to soak Mark at this juncture!)*
Marie:	He looked like something from outer space!
Graham:	... something very wet from outer space...
Mark:	Graham showed me a TV documentary... called **Just To Have Taken Part**. It had been made a few years earlier and told of his participation, as a skier(!) in the First Winter Olympics for the disabled. It wasn't all about skiing though... what struck me was the image of Graham using an electric drill, and then a circular saw, making his own bathroom cabinet... very impressive! It also showed Graham hacking an opponent's legs away from underneath him, in a blind football match... Graham beamed as the commentator quipped:
Marie & Graham:	"Graham is an Arsenal supporter."
Mark:	I liked his sense of humour...
Graham:	As a frequent visitor to Highbury, I've sometimes found it a blessing to be blind.
Mark:	Then he entertained me, long into the night, with his stories...
Graham:	I remember our Jack Russell stopping one time for a call of nature and taking an excessively long time. I tugged at the lead but he wouldn't budge. Other dogs arrived, growling. "Would they attack him?" I wondered. Strangely, none came closer. I tugged again at the lead... no response. Then someone ran by. "You won't move him for a little while friend!" I ran my hand down the lead, to find Ringer right on top of a bitch. They say that the dog is a man's best friend... on this occasion the roles were reversed... I put myself in his shoes and, although feeling pretty stupid, just stood there and waited while he indulged himself. *(Humour in this scene can easily be enhanced by two humans playing the two dogs!!!)*

Section 9

Mark: This was a man about whom we could write a play... the only question was, could we fit all his achievements into it? We had to... we just had to!

Graham: *(Slide[12] of Graham "looking" at the script with members of Epping Youth Theatre.)*
I was impressed by their energy and ideas, particularly that of using the actual words spoken in interviews, which helped to allay my fears regarding the quality of the script.

Mark: More than once I questioned our ability to see the project through... I don't think Graham and Marie were aware of those moments of self-doubt!

Graham: The effort they put into devising the play was comparable to that which a successful athlete needs.

Marie: We made many new friends amongst the Epping Youth Theatre.

Mark: The final scene of **Race** was to focus on whatever was to happen at the 1983 European Championships due to be held only a month or so before our Premiere!

Graham: An international gold medal was the one sporting achievement that had, so far, eluded me. This was probably my last chance to win one.

Marie: Although entered for the 100 metres, Graham's hopes rested on the 400 metres.

Graham: I had a brilliant relationship with my guide, Roger Wray, a top athlete from my club, at Haringey, who effectively sacrificed his own athletics career to train with me and help me achieve my goals.
(Show the slide[13] of Graham and Roger.)

Roger: We loved getting sharp and we loved getting in shape... Graham got himself into the shape of his life and me along with him.

Mark: You know this ending Gra? You mustn't feel under any pressure.

Graham: Not much!

Mark: Seriously... a broken leg would be equally dramatic!

---

(12) (13) These slides are available from MBA Literary Agents Ltd. See Footnote 2.

GRAHAM - World's Fastest Blind Man!

Graham: Thanks a lot!

Mark: Even losing... we'll make it work whatever happens!

Graham: I don't want to sit there watching myself lose night after night...

Roger & Graham: We both had a mission...

Roger: ... to win that gold medal.

Mark: We didn't know much about the competition but I couldn't conceive of anything other than him winning... it seemed "meant to be".
By the time Graham, Marie and Roger jetted off to Bulgaria, *Race to be Seen* was complete, bar the final scene. We were relying on Graham to create a fitting climax for us... it was all very dramatic... phoning his mum and dad after each race. First came the 100 metres:

Maud: It's not good Mark.

Mark: What happened?

Maud: He came ninth.

Mark: Ninth? Is he alright about it?

Maud: He's worried about the play...

Mark: Tell him not to be...

Maud: I did.

Mark: Good.

Maud: That's not all. Someone got his world record.

Mark: Seriously?

Maud: Yeh, a Russian... 11:38... he's not too bothered about that... but he was gutted at coming ninth.

Mark: Wish him good luck for the 400 tomorrow!
I replaced the receiver... I remembered Graham's parting words to me:

Graham: Everyone's saying I've got a good chance of the gold medal in the 400 and a bronze in the 100... I reckon I'll get a gold in both!

Section 9

Mark:	I hadn't ever seriously considered what would happen if he didn't give us the dream ending! I began to realise that an anti-climatic ending might not work... what were we to do? The next day I was back on the phone.
Maud:	He's through to the final of the 400's!
Mark:	Brilliant!
Maud:	He won the heat... 56.2
Mark:	Excellent.
Maud:	He said he's going for the world record.
Mark:	*(To audience.)* At that time it stood at 55.8. But what about the opposition... I remembered an interview we did before he left...
Graham:	Franzka, of Germany... his best time is 56.51... but he was absolutely knackered after it... in the same race, I did 56.6... but I had lots left... I can beat him... I know I can!
Mark:	In that same interview I asked him why he did it... his answer was immediate.
Graham:	I enjoy trying to win... that's what motivates me... some people reckon I'm trying to prove something... because I'm blind... that's rubbish... if I didn't enjoy it I'd never do it!
Mark:	Such events were never televised in those days... I wish they had been... I really wanted to see the race... to see if he could win. Obviously I know the result... but maybe you don't... so I hand you back to the final scene that Graham created for us in 1983... beginning with the night before that European Championship 400 metres Final.
Graham:	I felt very tired after the heats. I ached everywhere.
Marie:	Before we went to bed, the British Team Manager...
Mark:	... now famous for hosting the TV show Gladiators...
Marie:	... John Anderson, had said:
John:	The worst thing you can do Graham, is to run the final in your mind.

GRAHAM - World's Fastest Blind Man!

Graham:	Before going to sleep I put a Beatles cassette on... I remember thinking... they were the masters of music and tomorrow I should go out and prove that I was the master of the track. *(The cast sing quietly "Boy... you're gonna carry that weight... carry that weight... a long time" repeatedly under the following lines.)* I slept solidly until about two thirty, thinking about how I would start the race... my sleep was fitful after that.
John:	We were setting out to do something that had never been done before... to put British blind athletics right at the top of the world. Right at the heart of this was Graham... sparkling... leading the way as he always did... quietly, not with any great show... just solid determination to win a gold medal in the B1 400 metres.
Roger:	Breakfast was at seven.
Graham:	I couldn't eat a great deal.
Marie:	We arrived at the track at about eight o'clock...
Roger:	The sun was blazing down on Varna Stadium.
Marie:	Graham and Roger climbed to the back of the stands to find some shade.
John:	In 90 minutes Graham would know whether all the hard work would be rewarded.
Graham:	My legs still felt sore from the previous evening's semi-finals.
Marie:	He stretched out on a bench and tried to relax.
Roger:	We could hear the flags flapping in the wind and a buzz of conversation amongst the competitors and the spectators.
Mark:	Thoughts came flooding into Graham's mind with no rhyme nor reason. *(Possibly the cast could create still images depicting the events as they are described to animate the thoughts.)*
Maud:	Unconnected incidents... like, how as a child he had ridden his bike in Woodland Street.
Marie:	How in his youth he had dreamt of finding fame...

Section 9

Graham:	... and fortune...
Marie:	... as a rock star.
Roger/Harry	How he'd become the hero at Worcester College, getting himself thrown out for running bets.
John:	His meeting with Ron Murray, and that great night at Crystal Palace when he became the first blind person to run on equal terms against sighted athletes.
Marie:	On hearing that his name was to appear in *The Guinness Book Of Records* for his world record run.
Roger:	He thought of his friends at home...
Mark:	Of the Youth Theatre waiting eagerly for the result of this race before completing their play...
Marie:	His mum and dad...
Maud & Harry:	... waiting anxiously.
Marie:	He wondered where Marie was...
Mark:	Marie who had worked so hard, sacrificed so much for his success...
Maud:	... who always had the right words when things went wrong...
Mark & Maud:	... who was so completely dedicated.
Marie:	He knew how much a gold medal would mean to her.
Mark:	He had to win.
Graham:	I stood up to cheer Bob Matthews home in the 1500.
Roger:	Are you ready? *(The cast sing the line from the Beatles song powerfully once more slowing down the final syllables and holding the final note.)* *(Silence.)*
Graham:	I guess so.
Mark:	They started the long decent of the steps to the track and walked to the stadium car park to begin the warm up.
Graham:	My legs still felt tired...

GRAHAM - World's Fastest Blind Man!

Marie:	... that was worrying.
Roger:	We listened for the announcement to bring them to the track...
Graham:	... and I recalled the words of Betty Hill... widow of the World Champion racing driver...
Marie:	It takes sheer guts and courage to run when you are blind, let alone sprint like that. I compare it to my Graham getting into his racing car when he couldn't walk.
Announcer:	*(FX or through megaphone.)* Would athletes for the B1 Men's 400 metres final, report to the start immediately.
Graham:	We were drawn in lanes seven and eight... Roger, unlike the other guides, ran on the outside so we took up our position at the stagger for lane seven, with Roger in lane eight.
Marie:	I went over to cheer him on from the 200 metres mark... and then saw that... saw that there was something going on... between Graham, Roger and an Official.
Roger:	I run this side. We start here.
Official:	*(To Roger in broken English.)* You start here... him other side!
Roger:	I run this side!
Official:	Him lane eight... no argue... lane eight! Go to lane eight marker...
Roger:	*(Calmly.)* No... we stay here.
Official:	Must run other side of him...
Marie:	Then John got involved.
John:	Oy!!! What's going on here?
Roger:	They want me to run on the other side...
John:	He can't!
Official:	The others... they do this.
John:	They stay as they are...
Official:	They go to lane eight!

Section 9

John:	Not this way round... they start in lane seven!
Official:	Why you not understand? Start in lane eight!
John:	If you don't shut it... I'll make an official protest...
Official:	Go to lane eight I say.
John:	I'll have a word.
Graham:	What do we do?
Official:	If stay like that... I make report... they disqualify you... *(He starts to walk away.)*
John:	*(Chasing after him.)* You can't do this to athletes before a race!
Official:	I make report...
Roger:	Leave it John! We've got what we wanted. We can sort it out after.
Starter:	*(FX.)* Ona strt!
Graham:	Roger, who had been talking to John, was facing the wrong way!
Roger:	*(Turns. Makes as if starting the race from a standing position.)* Graham go forward a bit...
John:	*(Running behind Graham and Roger)* Protest! Protest! An official protest! Stop the race!
Starter:	*(FX.)* Gotozi
John:	Protest!
Graham:	For a split second, it flashed through my mind... should I stand up? Should I support John's protest?
John:	Stop the race!
Graham:	What was I meant to do?
John:	Protest!
Graham:	Almost instantly I told myself... don't be a fool... *(A starting pistol fires.)*
All:	Run!!!

GRAHAM - World's Fastest Blind Man!

Marie: Come on Gray!

(Marie and John shout encouragement to Graham. There are innumerable ways of staging this race... the guiding principals however, will be the same. The director/cast should be aiming to communicate the achievement... the excitement... the energy/ effort expounded.
I will go on to explain how after many attempts at this race scene I came to direct what I consider to be the most successful staging with Oaklands Youth Theatre some five years after the play was originally produced. This is offered by way of help rather than prescription. When Oaklands presented this play, we had a very large cast so this staging would have to be adapted if you are presenting this with a small group.
I was really keen to get the audience puffing and panting with the runners... I decided that they needed to "feel" the effort... to do this, I presented them with cast members actually tiring themselves out before their very eyes. Graham and Roger run in unison throughout the "race" in slow motion on a raised platform put in place specifically for this scene. Around them members of the cast do step-ups as fast as they possibly can until they are genuinely worn out. Simultaneously other members of the cast chorally shout a count of 1 - 55 (representing the number of seconds it took Graham to run the race) and Marie and John shout words of encouragement.
Gradually the step-up people drop out and sink to a sitting position trying to re-gain their breath/composure. I did this with the cast members initially to figure out who was the fittest... once this was established each cast member was given a number (that they could cope with) where they should drop out... the fittest dropping out out at about fifty-one. When fifty-five is reached everyone cheers. Graham and Roger adopt a victory pose with linked hands held aloft. Marie makes her way onto the podium as the cheering dies away.)

I couldn't see what happened at the end... did you win? Did you win?
(Silence.)

Section 9

Roger:	The race had been incredible... Graham had made a perfect start... coming out of the first bend he was already drawing away...
Marie:	I'd been calling him at the 200 mark... it'd looked good at that point...
John:	He'd taken down that back straight like a demented stag!
Graham:	I knew if I could hear anyone behind me on that final bend it was curtains for the gold medal...
John:	They'd presented a display of uniform running that I have never seen equalled.
Roger:	He just kept on running... past the line in fact...
Marie:	Well... did you win?
Graham:	Yeh... Course I did!
Marie:	Brilliant Graham! *(Hugging Graham)* I thought you had but didn't want to say till I was sure... *(Silence. The cast re-group.)*
Graham:	I didn't catch my time when it was announced... I was too wrapped up in the celebrations... the whole British team slapping me on the back... shaking my hand... offering me drinks... it was marvellous! I was sitting in the stands when I suddenly started to wonder what my time was. It had felt like one of the smoothest races I'd ever run... so I was really curious to find out... you can imagine... I had one hell of a shock when they told me... *(laughing)* they thought I knew! "What do you mean? No... I didn't hear any announcement!"
All (except Graham):	*(A melodramatic slow motion turn. Then animatedly:)* Fifty-five point five!
Marie:	A new world record! *(The action freezes.)*
John:	We'd achieved what we had set out to and it changed things forever. Along came others wanting to achieve at the highest level... and for the next decade or so Britain dominated blind athletics... winning everything... murdering the opposition... setting new standards.

GRAHAM - World's Fastest Blind Man!

	We won so many gold medals, the Bank of England wanted to employ us! That golden era began with Graham Salmon in Bulgaria. He was a real inspiration to me... to everyone. Britain should be proud of him.
Mark:	Back at home we were celebrating too... a dream ending from our Storybook man!
Announcer:	*(FX)* The medal ceremony for the B1 Men's 400 metres will take place now. *(FX with effects as though echoing in Graham's head.)*
Voice 1:	Totally blind for the rest of his life... we wondered how he was going to cope.
Voice 2:	I'm not unsympathetic but I want to be served by someone who can see...
Voice 3:	A blind person would be a severe drain on our sophisticated system...
Voice 4:	Oh! I'm afraid we don't employ blind people...
Voice 5:	I don't think *you'd* be able to manage the stairs.
Announcer:	*(Backed by suitably music. As this is said Graham bows his head to have John Anderson place around Graham's neck... a gold medal.)* And in first place... Graham Salmon of Great Britain... in a new World Record Time of 55.5 seconds.
Graham's Voice:	*(FX with echo. As this is being said Graham adopts a victory salute on his podium.)* Mark, I have some very grave news... they've got to take my leg away. *(Silence.)*
Mark:	When we finished ***Race To Be Seen*** a group of us went shopping to buy something for Graham to thank him for letting us tell his amazing story. We found just what we wanted in a joke shop... but it was closed. We hammered on the door... we were desperate. We explained to the shopkeeper what we wanted and why we wanted it. The magic of Graham Salmon worked again... the guy opened the shop and sold us the item. We were delighted!

Section 9

We knew Graham would really appreciate this. When we gave the little present to him I remember saying:
"We've found a very silly present for someone we've learnt can be a very silly man. I'm going to take your glasses away so that there can be no peeping before you open this..."
(Takes Graham's glasses off.)

Graham: *(Struggling to open the small box.)* I'm not very good at opening presents.

Mark: He opened it and, as the rest of the cast saw what it was, they fell about laughing. Graham put his hands inside to discover a joke pair of glasses with eyes on springs that come dangling down. He absolutely creased up!

Graham: *(Wearing the joke glasses.)* I always brought these glasses out at the end of my after dinner speeches... they always get a great reaction.
(Graham exits.)

Mark: I want to end this production by dimming the lights down... and letting you listen to an out-take of the last radio interview Graham did for Radio 4's 'In Touch'. It was about how he was determined to continue playing golf with his false leg... it'll leave you with the sound that was so much a part of the real Graham Salmon... Graham laughing.

(The lights dim to black and the out-take is played [14]. When it is finished the cast take a bow.)

THE END

---

(14) This out-take is on the CD available from dbda. See Footnote 1.

GRAHAM - World's Fastest Blind Man!

GRAHAM - World's Fastest Blind Man!

Top:
Graham at home, surrounded by his medals.

Bottom:
Graham with Mark 'reading' the Race to Be Seen playscript, in 1983.

The Songs of the Play

SONG 1:   RACE TO BE SEEN (1983)
            Words by Graham Salmon
            Music by Mark Wheeller

Mark:

Intro: E9   E   Emaj7   E6   B/E   A/E   E

        E9   E   Emaj7 E6   B/E   A/E   E
There's a race at the national stadi -um... all tickets have been sold.
  E9   E   Emaj7 E6   A/B   Amin/B   E
The world's top runners will be there... trying to take the gold.
D/E   E9   D/E   E
Their determination each to win mean that...
D/E   E   C/E   D/E E9   E   Emaj7 E6 B/E A/E E
We will witness a race to be seen.

Mark, Marie & Graham:

       E9   E   Emaj7 E6   B/E   A/E   E
There's a race at the local running track... no tickets to be sold.
   E9   E   Emaj7 E6   A/B   Amin/B E
There'll be no famous runners there... there'll be no winner's gold.
D/E   E   D/E   E
But their determination to succeed will surely mean
  D/E   E   C/D   D7
That they will be part of... a race to be seen.

All:

Gmaj7   Cmaj7   Gmaj7
Like the runners... we're all part of a race.
      Cmaj7   Gmaj7
Some days you win... some days you fall.
 Amin   Amin/G   D7/F#   D7
But if you never help yourself...   then you'll never win at all.
  Gmaj7   Cmaj7   Gmaj7   Cmaj7
If you spend your life just dreaming... success won't come to you.
Gmaj7   Cmaj7   A/B   B   E9 E Emaj7 E6 B/E A/E E
Race to be seen and show the world... what you can do!

Graham:

      E9   E   Emaj7 E6   B/E   A/E   E
There's a race we should all attempt to win... but we don't always try.

The Songs of the Play

     E9   *E*   *Emaj7* *E6*   *A/B*   *Amin/B* *E*
If we give up hope for the future now... this race of ours will die.

<u>Graham, Mark & Marie:</u>
   D/E   *E*   *D/E*   *E*
For life is like a relay... we have our lap to run
D/E   *E*   *C/D*   *D7*
Don't drop the baton... it's worth handing on!
<u>All:</u>
Gmaj7   *Cmaj7*   *Gmaj7*
Like the runners... we're all part of a race.
     Cmaj7   *Gmaj7*
Some days you win... some days you fall.
   Amin   *Amin/G*   *D7/F#*   *D7*
But if you never help yourself... then you'll never win at all.
    Gmaj7   *Cmaj7*   *Gmaj7*   *Cmaj7*
If you spend your life just dreaming...success won't come to you.
Gmaj7   *Cmaj7*   *A/B*   *B*   *E9 E Emaj7*
Race to be seen and show the world... what you can do!
E6 A/B *Amin/B* *E*   *Emaj7*   *E6 A/B* *Amin/B* *E*
  Race to be Seen.   **Race to be Seen.**

SONG 2:   **BREAKING LIVES (1983)**
             Words by Mark Wheeller & Steve Wyatt
             Music by Mark Wheeller

<u>Mark:</u>
Emaj7   *E7*   *A*   *Amin*
How can you tell this torment to your husband
        E   *A*   *B7*
When you haven't quite found the words to tell yourself?
Emaj7   *E7*   *A*   *Amin*
How can you find the terms that won't destroy him
    E   *Emaj7*
And speak them in tones that you can control yourself?
     A   *Amin*   *B B7*
Breaking news... breaking dreams... breaking lives.
Emaj7   *E7*   *A*   *C B7 Emaj7*
Where did she find the strength and the courage from?

GRAHAM - World's Fastest Blind Man!

Reprise

<u>Mark:</u>
Emaj7 E7   A   Amin
Think of the homes you know in town or country
  E   A   B7
And you'll see that this family here is just the same
Emaj7 E7 A   Amin
Like you or me they share in normal living
  E   Emaj7
But out of the blue this bolt breaks their pattern down.
    A   Amin   B7
Will their son now be scarred for the rest of his life... or even die?
Emaj7   E7   A   C B7 Emaj7 E7 A Amin B7 Emaj7
How will they face the problems the future holds?

SONG 3: KING OF THE COLLEGE (1983)

       Words & Music by Graham Salmon

E7   A
<u>Graham:</u>
  A
I was King of the College in my school day
 A
I organised the gambling to make it pay.
  E   D
A turf accountant paid me ten per cent commission
    E   D   A   E7
And I ran my own book on the chart positions.

   A
I'd meet with my friends in the library
A
Study the form and pick a horse or three
    E   D
For a year I took bets and avoided detection
<u>Mark:</u>
  E   D   A A7
He even won money on the General Election.

The Songs of the Play

<u>Graham:</u>
   D   A
Until the History teacher came snooping around.
   D   A
He caught me laying money with a bookie in town- he said:
<u>Teacher:</u>
D   A
"Gambling at your age is against the law!"
<u>Mark:</u>
  B7
He cancelled the bet...
<u>Graham:</u>
                   E7
... and the horse came in at nine to four!

    A
I was taken to the head and was promptly sent home...
<u>All:</u>
   A
The King of the College was kicked off his throne!
<u>Graham:</u>
   E   D
But the send off they gave me made the teachers frown
   E   D   A
And the bookie sent the money on... once all the fuss had died down!

SONG 4:   "MY WIFE" BY GRAHAM SALMON (1999)

        Words & Music by Graham Salmon

  Eb   Bb   Cmin7
<u>Graham:</u>
    Fmin   Bb
I have climbed many mountains reached many goals
       Fmin   Eb
And she's always been there beside me
  Fmin   Bb
She reaches out her hand and she touches my soul
    Fmin   Eb
And she gives all her love to guide me.

GRAHAM - World's Fastest Blind Man!

Ab   Eb
Always there behind the scenes
Ab   Bb
Never wanting the glory
Ab   Eb
Hope she knows how much she means...
Ab   Bb
Without her there's no story
  Eb Bb Cmin
Oh life... life is my wife

    Fmin   Bb
We have laughed in the sunshine and we've cried in the rain
    Fmin   Eb
And we've been through it all together
   Fmin   Bb
With a smile on our faces we can beat any pain
    Fmin   Eb
And we'll hold on to each other forever.

<u>All:</u>
Ab   Eb
Always there behind the scenes
Ab   Bb
Never wanting the glory
Ab   Eb
Hope she knows how much she means...
Ab   Bb
Without her there's no story
  Eb Bb Cmin
Oh life... life is my wife.

Other Plays by Mark Wheeller published by *dbda*

All plays are suitable for Youth Theatres, Schools, Colleges, and adult AmDram. They are ideal for GCSE Drama/English exam use and frequently do well in One Act Play Festivals. They offer both male and female performers with equally challenging opportunities.

> For enquiries or to order, please contact:
> **dbda**, Pin Point, 1-2 Rosslyn Crescent, Harrow HA1 2SB.
> Tel: 0870 333 7771   Fax: 0870 333 7772   E-mail: dbda@dbda.co.uk

All enquiries regarding performing rights should be made to: Meg Davis, MBA Literary Agents, 62 Grafton Way, London W1P 5LD. Tel: 020 7387 2076. E-mail: meg@mbalit.co.uk

---

Too Much Punch for Judy

ISBN 1 902843 05 3
KS4 to adult

Cast: 2m & 2f with doubling, or 3f, 3m & 6   **Duration:** 50 minutes

A hard-hitting documentary play, based on a tragic drink-drive accident that results in the death of Jo, front seat passenger. The driver, her sister Judy, escapes unhurt (or has she?). This play has become one of the most frequently performed plays ever!

'The play will have an impact on young people or adults. It will provoke discussion. It stimulates and wants you to cry out for immediate social action and resolution.'
Henry Shankula - Addiction Research Foundation, Toronto

Price: £ 4.95 per book *(order code TPJ SC)*
              £65.00 for a set of 15 *(order code TPJ SC15)*

Legal Weapon

ISBN 1 902843 01 0
KS4 to adult

Cast: 2m & 2f with doubling, or 1f, 3m & 13   **Duration:** 60 minutes

A fictional story using oral testimony of RTA offenders and victim families, Legal Weapon tells the story of a young man's relationship with his girlfriend – and his car. Both are flawed, but his speeding causes the loss of a life and the loss of his freedom. Fast, funny and very powerful.

'To write in the language of late teenagers is a fine example of high artistic accomplishment.'
David Lippiett, Guild of Drama Adjudicators

Price: £ 4.95 per book *(order code LW SC)*
              £65.00 for a set of 15 *(order code LW SC15)*

Why did the chicken cross the road?

ISBN 1 902843 00 2
KS 3&4

Cast: 2m & 2f with doubling, or 3f, 3m & 3   **Duration:** 35 minutes

The story of two cousins, Tammy and Chris. Tammy gets killed in a stupid game of 'Chicken' on the one morning that the cousins do not cycle to school. Chris, unable to tell anyone else about his part in the accident, has to live with this dreadful secret.

'An imaginative and moving look at risk taking at a time when peer pressure is at its strongest.'
Rosie Welch, LARSOA

Price: £ 4.95 per book *(order code WC2 SC)*
              £65.00 for a set of 15 *(order code WC2 SC15)*

Cast: 3f &2m with doubling, or 6f, 3m & 16   **Duration:** 70 minutes

This play is an adaptation of Maureen Dunbar's award winning book (and film) **Catherine** which charts her daughter's uneven battle with Anorexia and the family's difficulties in coping with the illness.

'This play reaches moments of almost unbearable intensity... naturalistic scenes flow seamlessly into sequences of highly stylised theatre... such potent theatre!'

Vera Lustiq - The Independent

ISBN 1 902843 08 8
KS3 to adult

Price: £ 5.50 per book *(order code HTS SC)*
£70.00 for a set of 15 *(order code HTS SC15)*

THE "WACKY SOAP" RANGE

A Pythonesque allegorical play (alcohol/tobacco/drugs). While washing with Wacky Soap leads to instant happiness and an inclination towards outrageous behaviour, prolonged use washes away limbs and ultimately leads to dematerialisation.

'This (play) gave every member of the large and energetic cast opportunities to shine... King Huff addressed his subjects from a Bouncy Castle, just one of the touches of visual humour in this fast, funny and thought provoking evening'.

Barbara Hart, Southern Evening Echo, Curtain Call Nominated "Best Production 2000"

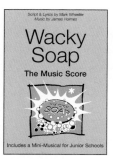

A 'past performance' CD gives you the opportunity to hear the songs of the play.

ISBN 1 902843 02 9
KS3 to adult
Duration: 80 mins
Cast: 6-100!
Includes follow-up work for KS3/4.

Price:
£ 4.95 per book
(order code WS SC)
£65.00 for a set of 15
(order code WS SC15)

ISBN 1 902843 06 1
A companion book containing the **Music Score** for all songs in the play and a **Mini-Musical** version for Junior Schools.

KS 3&4
Duration: 40 mins
Price:
£ 4.95 per book
(order code WS MSC)
£65.00 for a set of 15
(order code WS MSC15)

Price:
£15.00 each
(order code WS CD)

Also available is a fully orchestrated backing track CD.

Price:
£25.00 each
(order code WS BCD)

ISBN 1 902843 07 X
A fully illustrated book with the story of Wacky Soap in narrative form. It serves as an ideal (and quick) way of introducing the scheme of work, included in the full script.

Price:
£ 6.95 per book
(order code WS STB)
£90.00 for a set of 15
(order code WS STB15)

Other Plays by Mark Wheeller

Chunnel of Love

Script: Graham Cole & Mark Wheeller
Duration: 100 mins
Cast: 25 (11f, 8m & 6m/f)

A bi-lingual play (80% English & 20% French) about teenage pregnancy. Lucy is fourteen - she hopes to become a vet and is working hard to gain good grades in her GCSE exams, when she discovers she is pregnant. She faces a series of major decisions, not least of which is what to tell the father... Ideal as a school production and Key Stage 4 Drama course book.

Sweet FA !

Script: Mark Wheeller
Duration: 45 mins plus interval
Cast: 3f / 2m (or more)
Published by: SchoolPlay Productions Ltd. Tel: 01206 540111

A Zigger Zagger for girls (and boys)! A new play (also available as a full length Musical) telling the true life story of Southampton girl footballer Sarah Stanbury (Sedge) whose ambition is to play Football (Soccer) for England. Her dad is delighted ... her mum disapproves strongly! An ideal GCSE production and Key Stage 4 Drama course book. Drama GCSE scheme of work also available.

Blackout – One Evacuee in Thousands   MUSICAL

Script: Mark Wheeller with the Stantonbury Youth Theatre
Music: Mark Wheeller
Duration: 90 mins plus interval
Published by: SchoolPlay Productions Ltd.

A Musical about the plight of Rachel Eagle, a fictional evacuee in World War II. Rachel's parents are determined that the war will not split the family up. After refusing to have her evacuated in 1939 they decide to do so midway though 1940. At first Rachel does not settle but, after the death of her mother, she becomes increasingly at home with her billets in Northamptonshire. When her father requests that she return she wants to stay where she feels at home. An ideal large scale school production with good parts for girls (and boys).

The Most Absurd Xmas (Promenade?) Musical in the World...Ever!

Script: Lyndsey Adams, Michael Johnston, Stuart White & Mark Wheeller
Cast: Big!
Music: James Holmes
Duration: 100 mins
Published by: SchoolPlay Productions Ltd. Tel: 01206 540111

Eat your heart out Ionesco! If you want a musical with a message ... don't consider this one! Santa fails to arrive one year in the Bower of Bliss. Why not? A shortage of carrots perhaps? Or is it because the central character is forbidden to use her musical gift, and whose parents disguise her as a cactus? It all ends reasonably happily and is a bundle of laughs. Originally conceived as a Promenade production. An ideal large scale school Christmas production or alternative an "absurd" summer production.

For more details and an up-to-date list of plays, please visit Mark's website:
www.amdram.co.uk/wheellerplays (please note wheeller has two "l")

All enquiries regarding performing rights should be made to: Meg Davis, MBA Literary Agents, 62 Grafton Way, London W1P 5LD. Tel: 020 7387 2076. E-mail: meg@mbalit.co.uk